MARKETING SIMPLIFIED

AN EXPERIENCE-BASED, STEP-BY-STEP GUIDE TO GROW SALES

TED J. MARENA

Pro Indie Publishing

www.proindiepublishing.com

Book cover designed by Terri Dilley

Author image photographed by Gregory Checchi

Book formatted by Jennifer Eaton

CONTENTS

PREFACE

Everything I've learned and experienced is in this book. Based on my extensive marketing and sales experience, I've created 7 steps one should take to execute a successful marketing promotion. This book is not leveraging any research or university study; I'm drawing on more than 25 years of sales, business development and marketing experience. If you are looking for a direct plan to promote and market your product or service, this book is for you. There is no pontification or needless background data to get the point across. This book is short because I get right to the point. It is intended to explain, in an organized step-by-step manner, how to promote your product, service, idea or yourself. There are only 7 steps to follow, and you can do them!

The reality is there are numerous types of marketing: digital, strategic, product, promotional, tactical, etc. This book is focused on the best ways to promote and implement outbound marketing. Outbound marketing is the focus on promoting a product or service to the widest possible audience. This is what most people think of when you say that you do marketing. All of the key information I've learned is shared in *Marketing Simplified* to help you promote your product, service, ideas or yourself and become the most successful you can be.

If you are a professional doing product or technical marketing or marketing communications and you want to improve your skills, this book will prove invaluable in that endeavor. In addition, small business owners, self-employed individuals, agency representatives and consultants will benefit greatly from the information presented. C level executives and marketing leaders will also gain new insight into what their teams really need in order to achieve successful campaign execution. Perhaps the individuals who will be helped the most are those who do not know the first thing about marketing. There is something for everyone in *Marketing Simplified: An Experience-Based, Step-by-Step Guide to Grow Sales.*

INTRODUCTION TO THE MARKETING SIMPLIFIED STEPS

YOU DON'T JUST DO MARKETING

I find it peculiar that everybody thinks they can do marketing. I've heard from many people who seem to think marketing is easy to do and that no training is needed. Perhaps it's because you don't have to have excellent mathematics skills or know physics or some other technical background. The reality is marketing is a proficiency that has to be mastered just like any other career skill. The good news is that I've simplified what you need to do to market and promote well. Let me share a real story first just to explain why this book will be valuable to you.

Figure 1. Marketing is not easy, but with this book, it is simplified and you can do it!

A couple of years ago a technical nonprofit organization needed a marketing leader. This individual was going to be elected by the members of the group. The individual who won the election was a software engineer. He ran for the position because he thought it would be fun and easy to do. I was surprised to find out what little direction and knowledge the new marketing leader had about what marketing professionals should do.

I supposed I should not have been surprised given he was a software engineer. After all, I didn't know how to program in C or Python software languages either. What was clear was that he had run for the position not understanding what was required to be successful. After we worked together for a couple of months, he stepped down and then suggested the organization appoint me the marketing leader. This story was shared not to proclaim only marketing backgrounds are qualified to do marketing. The point is that marketing is not something you approach mindlessly. I was inspired to write this book to help others. If you don't know how to get started or what should be done to grow sales or you just want to improve your marketing capabilities, keep reading.

This book will help you market yourself, your product or service. More specifically I will be focusing on outbound marketing. Although I have done technical, product, tactical, and strategic marketing, my passion, and the focus of this book, is outbound marketing. Outbound marketing is the focus of promoting a product or service to the widest possible audience. Whether you are marketing your own business, a product, service, solution or idea, the information I'll share will be a great guide for you. It doesn't guarantee success, nobody can do that, but you will absolutely improve your odds of success if you follow the Marketing Simplified steps.

. . .

What will be shared with you is all based on my actual work experience of being in many marketing roles, business development and sales positions. I'll be walking you through the steps necessary for you to execute the best possible marketing campaign, as well as how to best promote your product, idea or service. One last diversion before we jump into the Marketing Simplified steps, I want to share with you one of the reasons I excel at marketing.

TURN MY WEAKNESS INTO YOUR STRENGTH

If you know me well, then you are aware of what the number 410 represents. No, it is not a Chinese number sequence or anything culturally related. 410 represents the score I earned when I took my English SAT test. The SAT was a standardized test taken just before university enrollment. 410 is not considered a good score by any measure. One of my good high school friends regularly reminds me that they give you 200 points just for signing your name. I always struggled trying to under-stand or construct complex English phrases. Why am I sharing this supposed weakness of mine with you? Well, this "weakness" is one of the reasons why my marketing programs have been successful. Whenever I communicate in the English language, I always keep it simple, because I have to! Big, fancy words or phrases were not something I could relate to or easily understand. I am always looking to simplify sentences, simplify messages, simplify tag lines and so on. If a message is simple, people will understand it and become interested to learn more.

Of course simplifying your message is only one part of promoting your product or service. Let's jump into the Marketing Simplified steps. There are seven steps in the process. Some will be easier for you than others, but all can be accomplished. First, we start with goal setting. Believe it or not when you do marketing, it absolutely should have goals. Actually it is essential to set at least one goal. Then I'll explain messaging in detail and how to set up an impactful top line message for your product or service.

Once you have the messaging set, your collection of marketing material, also known as collateral will be created. What specific collateral you need to create will be defined when you map out what you will deliver. This is a map or plan detailing what you will actually do. All your collateral will echo and amplify your messaging as we will see later. The next step is what I often referred to as "herding the cats". Consider this aligning the organization to ensure everybody is rowing in the same direction. This is important if you are in an organization or larger company. If you are in a smaller company then this step will be quicker for you. Then comes the delivery: what you're going to do, how you're going to do it and who is going to do it. The last step is measuring your marketing efforts. All marketing campaigns should be measured against the original goals that were set. By doing this you will be able to make adjustments and continue your sales progress.

To summarize, here are the steps we will take.

- Setting your goal(s)
- Messaging
- Mapping out your delivery
- Building your collateral
- Herding the cats
- Delivering
- Measuring

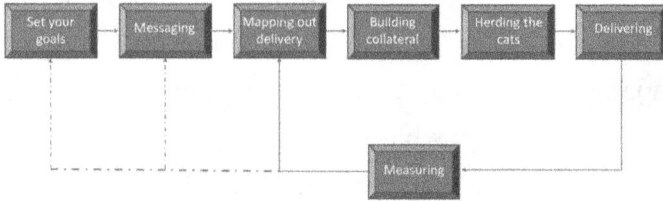

Figure 2. Visual representation of the Marketing Simplified
steps

Crystal Clear: Don't worry if you are
inexperienced in marketing. You can implement
these steps. In addition to various examples I will
use throughout the book to assist you, I am also
going to demonstrate how a fictitious sole
proprietor jewelry maker, Crystal Clear, would
implement the Marketing Simplified steps in each
chapter.

2

SETTING YOUR GOALS

BELIEVE THAT YOU HAVE TO BRING REVENUE IN

Before we begin, I want you to recall a campaign that you think is memorable, creative or impactful. Is it a Superbowl commercial or an Apple product reveal or some social media advertisement? Whatever you are remembering is likely the same impression and feeling that you will want to create in your audience. Following the steps I have laid out can help you get to that result. Will you change the world? Most likely not, but your product, service or message will be improved by the knowledge I'm sharing.

The first step before you begin to market anything is determine one or more goals. If you work for a large corporation your goal should probably align with revenue generation. If you have your own business, you already know this. You should develop a mindset that the business survival is dependent on you and that you can be the difference that will bring in the revenue. At the end of the day marketing just to do marketing makes no sense, it is a waste of time. You need to set a goal or two for what you are promoting.

CREATE A SALES FUNNEL

Often creating a sales funnel can help you set a goal. A sales funnel is often described as the ideal path that a consumer takes to become a customer. To help you out, here is an example of a goal I had for a product campaign. We were introducing a new product and we wanted to achieve $25M in sales in four years. This product required that engineers adopt it, integrate it with their end product, test it and then ultimately, ship it. We knew there were many steps, and it would take some time before we would achieve revenue recognition. Our sales cycle took time to develop and we took that into account. We also knew that each customer, on average, would purchase $100K once they were in production. So we knew we had to win 250 customers. ($25M / $100K).

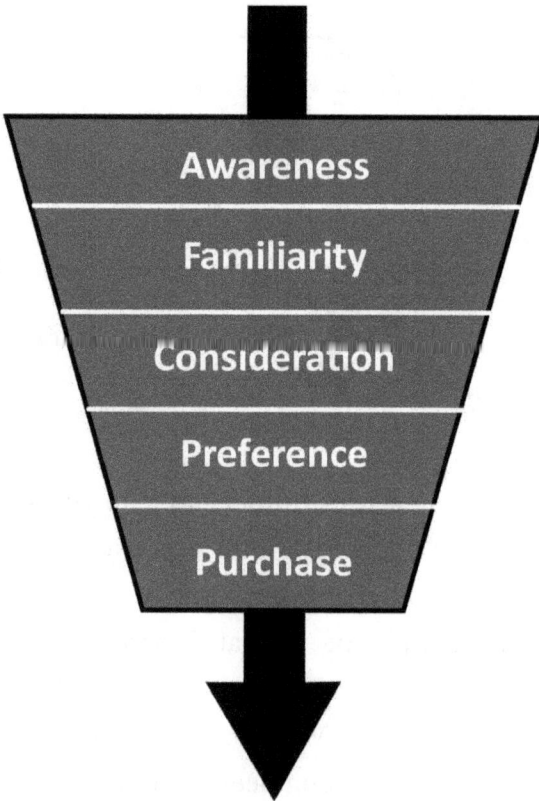

Figure 3. Typical sales funnel

How do we win 250 customers? As you can imagine, we had to show our product to a much larger number of engineers because not all were going to use our product.

Our historical conversion rate was about 20%. To clarify, let me explain what I mean by conversion rate. For example, for every five customers we engaged with on our product, we would win one. So we needed to create a campaign that worked with our sales team to promote our product to 1250 customers, (250 x 5). This was our minimal goal, 1250 customer opportunities. By getting to at least this number we had a path to ultimately earn $25M. Often, if our campaign was going well, we would increase our goals further to better improve our odds of success.

Crystal Clear: Our fictitious jewelry maker has recently figured out a way to make various jewelry pieces out of what looks like sea glass. Sea glass begins as broken bottles and pieces of glass tossed into the ocean. It is tumbled and smoothed by the waves and currents, and normally takes 7-10 years to become smooth and well-glossed. Crystal has figured out a way to make sea glass quickly and very cost effectively. She wants to sell it as a new product in her online store. She currently sells about $4,000 worth of other jewelry products per month.

How would Crystal go about setting her marketing goals? Based on her experience, she believes the average selling price for each sea glass jewelry will be $25. This is very similar to the pricing for her other jewelry lines. Since she can make about 25 pieces a week, or 100 per month, she decides her goal should support this production level. Attaining 100 customers per month x $25 yields $2500 per month. A goal of 100 customers per month can be attained with a goal further up the sales funnel. Crystal needs to make more than 100 people aware every month to achieve her goal. She checks her website visitor statistics and finds out that on average, four thousand visitors go to her site. Since the new sea glass line is priced similarly, her goal should be to increase website visits by at least 2.5 thousand per month. Crystal decides this will be her funnel goal for the new sea glass line.

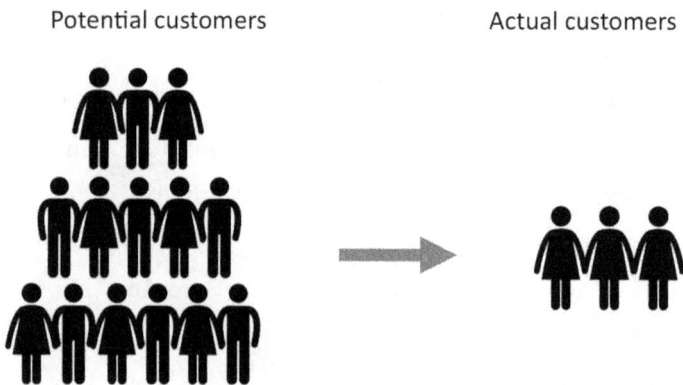

Potential customers

Actual customers

Figure 4. Setting your goal visualization

The goal that you set may be completely different. You may want to achieve a certain number of website visits or generate a specific number of leads or increase awareness by hitting a social media following goal. Take a bit of time and think through what goal or goals you want to have for your marketing campaign. In your business today, how do you convert customers? How many prospects do you need? If you are struggling with how to define a goal, imagine that your marketing campaign is over. What does success look like? At the end of the campaign how would you, your boss, or others view the result as a positive achievement? Work backwards from the sales goal to create your key marketing goals.

If you work in an organization that has sales people or reps, you need to think about what will help them when you set a goal. We will share more details about collaborating with sales later in the book. Overall, when you are promoting something you generally think in terms of a funnel. Think of it this way. I have to make so many people aware of my product or service. Of those, there will be a certain number that are interested enough to become familiar. A percentage of those will consider what you are offering. A subset of these individuals will choose to purchase it. One of these milestone numbers is likely a candidate for your marketing goal.

ARE YOU INTRODUCING TROMBONE OIL?

A word of caution before we proceed. At this point, take a deep breath and ask yourself a tough question, "Is what I am promoting trombone oil?" I recall reading a line similar to this from Bob Iger, the former CEO of Disney.[1] The point is that, although there is a market for trombone oil, the quantity sold every year is very small. In thinking about the campaign you are putting together, ask the difficult questions, and explore the market potential for your product/service. This will help you set realistic goals and appropriate expectations.

. . .

If you work in a large company, you may not have a choice to change everyone's thinking. Figuratively speaking, I once promoted trombone oil. A previous company I worked for had many business units, or BUs. There was a solution that I noticed which used devices from two BU's and the software from a third. No one company could provide a complete solution. At the time, I thought we could package this and promote it as an all-in-one solution. My marketing mind was thinking that we could win a majority of these designs, because everything was within our one company and customers would find this valuable. All of this was true, but the reality is there were only a very, very small number of customers who needed this.

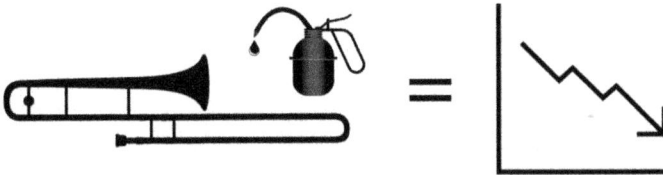

Figure 5. Avoid selling "trombone oil"

Looking back, I wish I had asked more difficult questions about this solution. I didn't know enough about the entire market opportunity. It may have been that I was afraid the answer was to not promote this at all. That is the conclusion I should have drawn. When one of the BUs only assigned a junior software engineer to the project, it should have been a huge red flag. They were just happy to have a marketing person in another BU, me, promote their technology with minimal effort from their side. A lesson was learned and I just moved on.

To recap, set at least one goal for your campaign. Please don't skip this step and just start marketing or promoting. Without some goals against which to measure, you will have no idea what impact you are having. With at least one goal, you can now begin to think about the different collateral you will create. Get excited about the journey. You've completed the first step and are on your way.

3

CREATING YOUR MESSAGING

ALL THE CONTENT WILL ECHO YOUR TOP LINE

Now that you have at least one goal, we can move onto messaging. Don't move to this step without some goals established. Remember, you don't just want to market for marketing's sake. The message creation is what I consider one of the hardest parts of the Marketing Simplified steps. Coming up with the messaging is critical and sometimes very difficult. Your message is the key part of your product or service story. Ultimately, you should envision promoting your offering as if you were telling a story. Your messaging is the opening statement, and you add more details and aspects as your promotional campaign moves forward. I can't emphasize enough how important it is to nail the messaging. Why, you ask?

Simply stated, the messaging is the point from which the collateral, brochures, banners, images, websites, social media, videos, etc should flow. Think of the messaging as the top of the pyramid, and everything that you create is informed by it. The top level message is king. All your collateral should echo the messaging that you create. Your message could be a single brand name or a short sentence or both.

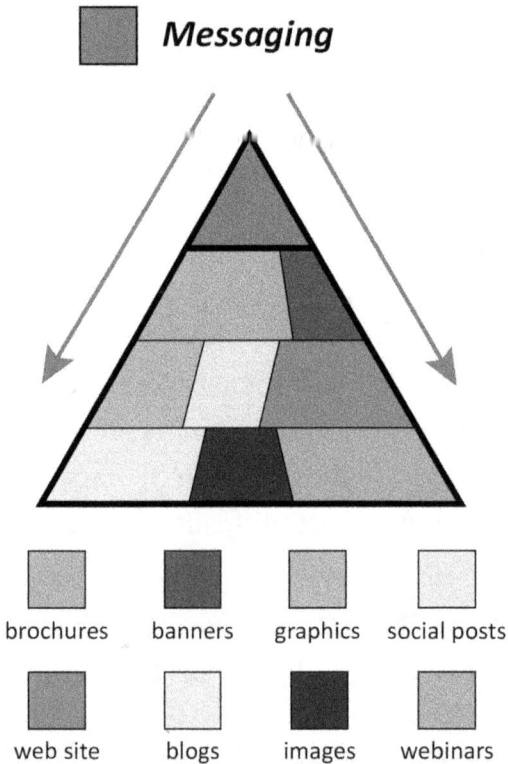

Figure 6. Messaging is the key to your story

When you work to create your messaging, you can start a number of different ways. For example, you can start by listing product benefits, product attributes/capabilities, emotions your product or service engenders, etc. Another option is to have a more abstract message that ties to your brand/product/service but is still relatable. When in doubt, my suggestion is to create a message that explains your product. Imagine you were in an elevator with a large potential client. The bell dings and the door is about to open, the client is about to walk out, what one line would you say about your product/service to get their attention?

An example messaging line is what we developed earlier in my career at a technology company. We were introducing a semiconductor device also known as a chip. The message line was, "Our devices are lowest power, cost-optimized, and mid-range density." Another example was, "Achieve higher levels of integration, security and reliability." Obviously both of these messages are for high tech products and aimed at a technical audience. The message line for both these products is meant for an engineer who is the target client. These short phrases make it very clear what the key attributes and benefits of the product are.

Using product attributes will not be for everyone. If you are marketing a service, you may want to point out what differentiates you from others, or what is your unique focus. An architecture firm may be "your forever home designer." A consultant may want to emphasize "reducing your anxiety by handling your toughest tasks." When you are starting, write down all the decent sounding ideas. Brainstorm and don't limit yourself at the beginning. Often your messaging may come out of multiple lines.

Crystal Clear: Our jewelry maker kicks the idea around about an abstract message for the new sea glass line. After talking to friends, her brother, who helps her in the business, and other industry contacts, she decides against this. Her initial messages included "Wearable art just for you" and "Bring the beach with you wherever you go." Ultimately, she decided to name the product line "Sea Glas" to ensure that the customer understood the product was not from the sea but had the same characteristics. For her message, she chose, "Sea glass jewelry for every occasion." It clearly states what the product is and when it can be worn. Crystal wanted a simple message so clients would quickly understand her new jewelry line.

Your messaging does not have to be about *what* you are offering, but *why* you are offering. Does your organization have an environmental impact goal, or is it socially responsible and giving back to the community? Was there some historical importance to the business or cause that is central to the company culture? Is there a family tradition that makes your company unique? Consider integrating the "why you are doing business" in your messaging.

You can look to other companies in completely unrelated fields for inspiration. Maybe your product or service is associated with, or complementary to, other markets; you might be able to use pieces from those other organizations. Often there are companies that you respect or admire. What is their messaging headline? What sentence or phrase do others use in their promotions? Look all around for ideas to utilize for your messaging.

Figure 7. Be creative when you are generating your messaging

Depending on how well known your brand is and how much budget you have, you might also tailor your messaging to elicit a feeling. A great example is Subaru.

Every commercial they make fails to mention the engine or any specifications about the car. Rather, the messaging centers around family and love. They can do this because for years everyone has known they offer four-wheel drive sedans and wagons. Their vehicles were often seen off-road. To differentiate from other manufacturers, they changed their messaging from one highlighting product attributes to one designed to elicit a warm feeling associated with love and family. This type of messaging may not be the right path for you, but be open and creative, especially at the early stages of creating your messaging.

ASK FOR OUTSIDE INPUTS

I'd also encourage you to include other people when you are working on your messaging. First, work with a few others who know your product or service well. Then you should engage a wider group of individuals and ask for their ideas. It is always beneficial to receive input from a variety of sources. Be sure to get the opinions of a diverse range of individuals, including those that may not be familiar with your type of product or service. Be vulnerable and accept constructive criticism. The best messaging is often created when many viewpoints are considered. I once had to modify a brand name that sounded like "without, hollow or absent" in another language. We discovered this when we talked to someone who grew up in the Middle East. Although our group loved the name and what it represented in English, we agreed to abandon it because it was a global product. You may recall in the 1970s that General Motors introduced a car called the Chevy Nova, which literally means "no go" in Spanish. How many do you think they sold in Mexico?

The key with your message is to keep it succinct. Making it memorable is always a plus, but most important is to drive across the key points of your brand/product/service or the feelings you want associated with it. Once you have your messaging, you should promote it inside your own company. Everyone in the organization should know your messaging headline. For example, IBM has the headline, "Unlock the Value in Your Organization with Watson." Pizza Hut says, "Nobody Out Pizzas The Hut." What you ultimately want is for all your employees to recite your message when someone asks, "Hey what is our new product/service?" The response is your messaging. The individuals who have been working on your offering will want to know, and others in the company should as well. Of course for sales, this will be very important once you launch the campaign.

. . .

We'll discuss details later about how to create your content, but honestly your collateral will be easier to create once you have the messaging finalized. This is why I emphasize the importance of messaging. All your collateral will echo your headline. How, where and when you deliver the various collateral is the next priority to tackle.

___

4

MAPPING OUT YOUR DELIVERY

THE HOW, WHERE AND WHEN

Now that you have your goal(s) and messaging set, the next step is to map out how, where and when you will deliver your story. Some marketing individuals might suggest the next step is to begin creating the collateral for the campaign, but I disagree. As a reminder, collateral is everything your customers need in order to learn about, understand and use your product/service/idea. In my experience, figuring out all the ways you want to promote your product or service should be the next step. Knowing the different ways you want to get your messaging and your story out, will dictate the exact collateral material you need to be creating. It is assumed that you have a good idea of your target customers. Is your product for a broad audience or only a dozen companies? Obviously the details of your campaign will be influenced by who you want to obtain as a customer. Keep this in mind when you think about the medium you will be using.

Another key point for you at this stage is to be open and think creatively. One important lesson which helped me in my career was understanding the definition of insanity to mean doing the same things over and over again and expecting different results. Let that sink in, because it was career changing for me. If what you were doing in the past was not yielding the desired results, then stop doing it! Don't be afraid to try new things. If your past results were not what you wanted, then do something else. Don't follow the rule of insanity. Look around at how competitors and completely unrelated companies are doing their marketing. Sometimes the best ideas are modified from what you see elsewhere. Do some searching for inspiration and you will see it is often easier to modify than to create.

Figure 8. Be open and don't follow the rule of insanity

An additional key fact is that repetition is required to have your message received. Accept that, for someone to absorb what you're promoting, it will require that they see or hear it multiple times. You can find all kinds of studies about repetition and how often someone needs to see or write something to remember it. In today's fast-paced world, where information is flying at us constantly, the number of repetitions for someone to remember is likely higher than most studies. Regardless of what it is for each individual, realize you have to deliver your message multiple times and numerous different ways.

DETERMINE THE FREQUENCY

Start by writing down all the different ways that you could think of to promote yourself, product/service, etc. Many common examples include your website, social media, industry events, blogs, videos, contributed articles, podcasts, meetup groups, webinars, search campaigns, conferences, press releases, free samples, classes, etc. Don't be afraid to come up with out-of-the-box ideas. After all, some products are sold in a door-to-door methodology. Tupperware was sold by having parties at one's house. Who would have thought that would be successful?

Figure 9. Different media are key to allow your
message to sink in

Crystal Clear: For Crystal, her website is paramount for success but she is open to thinking of new ways to attract customers. To date, she has primarily used search engines and social media to attract visitors to her website. She plans to continue with these but will also create a video about herself, her motivations and why she is making jewelry. Crystal will also go to pop-up craft markets, conduct a livestream with an artisan clothing company and raffle off an original sea glass jewelry piece for all those who agree to receive emails from her. All the mediums she uses will be arranged in a chronological manner to achieve a regular cadence of her Sea Glas "Sea glass jewelry for every occasion" message.

Now let's talk about how to schedule and coordinate the communication of your message. Most importantly, you want to create a marketing campaign that has a regular drum beat. By this I mean that you should plan on regularly scheduled promotion. The campaigns I have spearheaded have often kicked off with a bang and then kept going for months, similar to the way a lightning strike is followed by rolling thunder. For example, you might have a new product reveal that you put on your website and also create a press release. This is the lightning and all the promotional actions you follow up with in the days, weeks and months afterward is the rolling thunder.

LEVERAGE THE SWIM LANES

What I have found most helpful is a slide or two that conveys all the activities that the campaign will encompass. The best representation I have found is to use the swim lane chart. This is one or maybe two pages that explains all the various activities you will do to promote your product, service or idea.

At the very top is a calendar layout that could be in weeks, months or quarters. Basically what you want to do is list the calendar anchor points on the first row or two and then all of the activities that you plan to do in the rows below. The top row might be events or press releases, whatever is going to be the kick off for your marketing promotion. If you don't have any major event, then you should put calendar fixed items at the top that are natural events to trigger marketing promotions. For example, you might list new product features, updated software enhancements, new expected services, etc.

Marketing Plan through 2H CY 2022

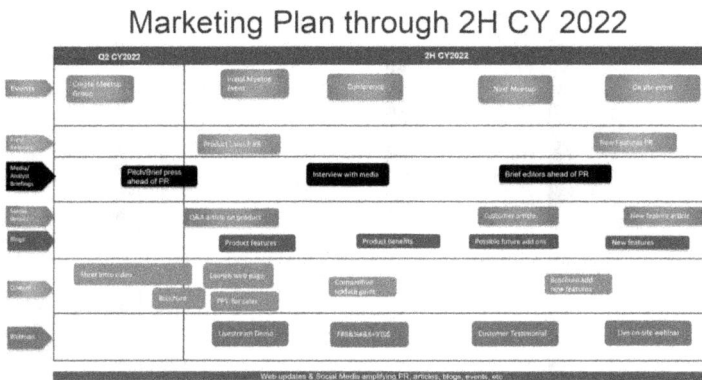

Figure 10. Swim lane example for Q2 - Q4 2022. Enlarged image shown on following page.

The next several rows will be the categories of where you are going to deliver your collateral. There is no rigid method for these rows. You might get very specific, such as a row for your web site, every social media channel, blogs, etc. My advice is to list rows that remind you what is needed, but don't make the sheet or sheets overwhelming to consume. In that light, you may want to combine all your social media together in one lane.

List the various rows for all the different mediums you plan to use. As a reminder, earlier in this chapter we listed websites, social media, industry events, blogs, videos, contributed articles, podcasts, meetup groups, webinars, search campaigns, conferences, press releases, free samples, classes, etc.

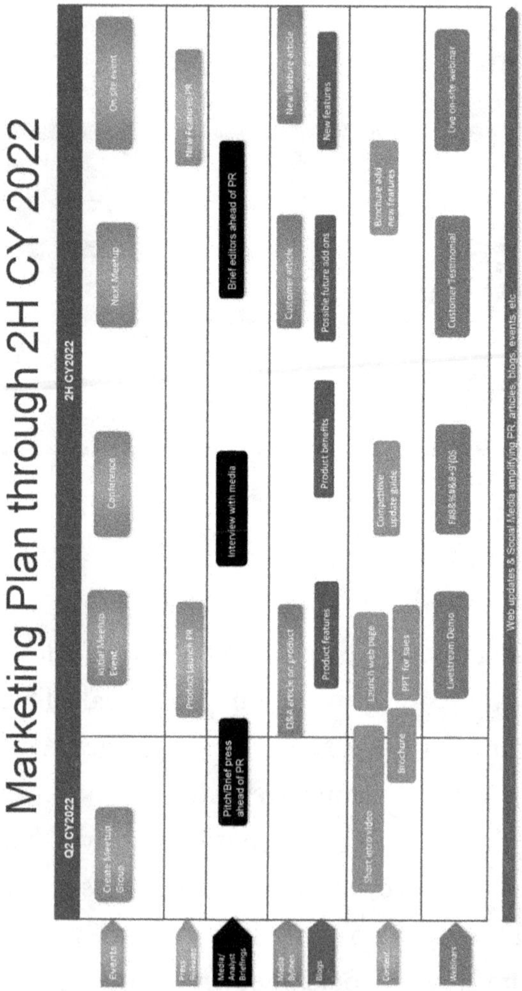

Figure 10.1. Enlarged swim lane example for Q2 - Q4 2022.

You can group some of these together to simplify the chart or add your own groupings or ideas. Ultimately you want to be confident when you look at the sheet that it clearly shows what you will be doing and when.

To save you time, you can purchase and download my swim lane template power point presentation which has examples of swim lanes. This file also includes a simplified template of slides that you can use to communicate your marketing campaign to others, including your boss and executives. I will explain further in the "Herding the Cats" section why this is valuable. The power point presentation has all the template slides and swim lane examples. It is easy to use this as a starting point to modify for your marketing campaign. Purchase this file through PayPal.

Click paypal.me/marketingsimplified/2.99 to send me the funds and complete the transaction. The swim lane template PPT will save you time and make it easier to visualize and communicate your campaign. For only $2.99 the PowerPoint file will be emailed to your address.

Don't obsess over the swim lane categories. What you need is the calendar at the top, then the anchor events, product introductions and below that, the various medium categories. Once you have that, then you can start to fill in the various campaigns or collateral that you will be producing. All of the different promotional tasks you are planning will each echo your messaging. When your collateral is created in the next chapter, each piece will reinforce the message of your product/service. What you want to do is add to the pile at this point. Repetition in reaching your audience with a consistent message is how you will drive your story home.

Now recall how I impressed upon you the importance of having a goal? Well here is where it is needed to tie things together and guide the actions you will execute. Now, whatever your goal is, you need to make some assumptions and break things down by marketing activity. You can use a simple spreadsheet.

For example, let's say you have a goal of 500 leads by some specific date. You make assumptions for each of the activities. For a webinar you might assign 50, a brochure created may be 20 registrations, a meetup or conference could be 35 and so on. My suggestion is to be very conservative about assigning leads to social media posts. I often think of these as make up for other areas that fall short or help you exceed your goals. Remember, it takes multiple times for people to remember your product/service, so it would be more realistic to have fewer leads in the early campaigns and then increase as you move forward. Your first webinar might only generate 25 leads but the next one 3 months later might bring 50.

If you want to move up earlier in the sales funnel for your campaign, you might assume that a certain number of post views or web page visits will nurture into a lead. Suppose that for every 25 views you think you can average 1 lead, then you could create goals for views as well. Don't go crazy creating more goals, but do create these smaller goal assignments so you can see your progress once you get the campaign going.

Plan on over-subscribing to your goal once you fill in each entry. Remember, people are busy. They are not just waiting for your campaign. So set goals that are a stretch but achievable.

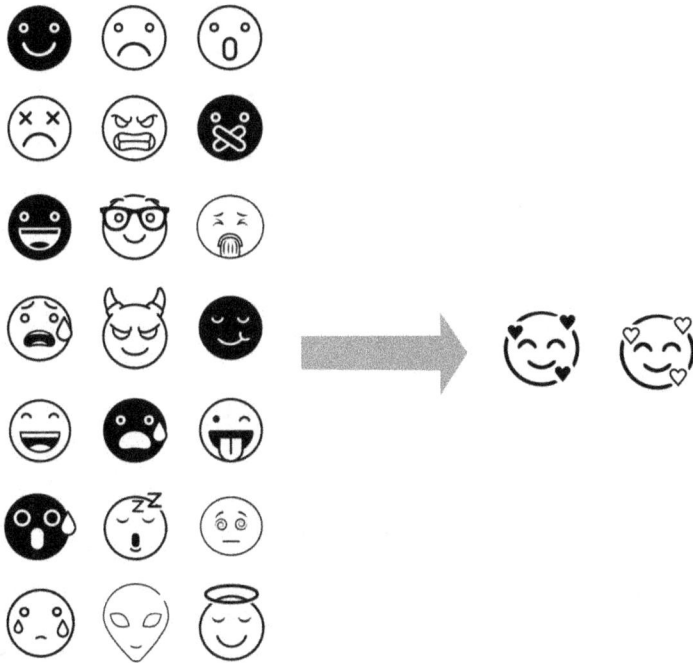

Figure 11. Reach more individuals to hit your goals

Use multiple methods to get your message out. It will take you longer to reach people than you think. Go beyond what you think you need to do to increase your odds for success. My suggestion is to list out all of the details on a swim lane page or multiple pages. Depending on the scale of what you are doing, you may not want to call out every detailed post or activity in the swim lane chart.

THE IMPORTANCE OF SEARCH

The point is to write down all the collateral you will be creating and when, as well as in what medium you plan on delivering it. Speaking of medium, I'd suggest you strongly lean on search engines, your website and videos for whatever you roll out. I'm not sure why, but more marketing professionals seem to be fixated on social media. Every study that I've seen shows social media is a much smaller influencer than search engines, your website and videos. This recent article[2] mentions 87% of buying decisions begin by searching. I'm not saying to forego everything other than search, your website and videos, but just ensure these are a key part of your messaging campaign.

. . .

One thing to consider is this: I've worked with many marketing professionals who think they cannot start a campaign until they have a product in hand. My experience says this does not need to be the case. If your company has a hard rule of not starting promotions until the product/service is ready, then tow the line. However, if you have flexibility, you can start promoting earlier. The key is to not start so early that you excite people and can't deliver within a timely manner.

If the product/service you are delivering has a long lead time or lengthy negotiation process, then you should consider starting your campaign before all the product/service deliverables are ready. For example, we were introducing a product in a new technology that required customers to change their software infrastructure. This was not something decided overnight, and the actual conversion took months once it was started. We decided to kick off a campaign focusing on the technology, the benefits of it to the customer and so on. We did not talk about the actual product until 6 months after the start of the campaign. This allowed us to spread awareness, start building interest and generate customer meetings to better fill our sales funnel.

. . .

Lastly, not to get overly specific, but you should always plan to put out your messaging between Monday just before lunch time to Thursday afternoon. This is the most likely time to grab people's attention[3]. Your industry may be vastly different, but from my experience, the majority of organizations put their content out during the referenced time frame. Individuals tend to look for business information more during the Monday just before lunch to Thursday afternoon time frame. Of course, if your product is targeted for night owls, weekend use or has other unique characteristics, you should alter when to put out your content.

5

BUILDING YOUR COLLATERAL

THE CONTENT WILL ECHO YOUR MESSAGING

With your goals set, messaging done and a plan on where, when and how you will deliver your story, you can now start creating your collateral. When I talk about collateral, I am referring to all types of items. Collateral could be multiple graphics, a web page banner, a product brochure, images, evaluation units, videos, drawings, pictures, web site forms, samples, how to guides, etc. Collateral is everything that your customers need in order to learn about, understand, and use your product/service/idea.

Use your messaging headline, and ensure that it is prominent in all you create. Notice that I said prominent and not front and center. You want to reinforce what it is that differentiates your product/service. Each piece of collateral does not have to have your messaging as the headline, however everything should weave your messaging tag line somewhere in it. Let your messaging be the guide that drives the creation for your collateral. For some of your collateral you may want to emphasize the more specific attributes and other pieces you may want to be higher level or focus more on the benefits. Overall you should have the messaging woven throughout the vast majority of what you create.

Here are a few more tips when you create your collateral. Use fewer words and more images, diagrams and pictures. People don't have vast amounts of spare time. You need to communicate your message as quickly as possible. You want a clean look, and less text will be important for overall attractiveness. More technical products/services will require text, but work diligently to have the initial cover page convey your message with minimal text and informative images. Of course you will leverage your tag line, company logos and other graphics to convey your story. In larger organizations you likely have templates to guide you, but for smaller companies, you may not. This is an opportunity to create templates and standardize your look and feel which will allow you to create future collateral more quickly.

LOOK AT THINGS LIKE YOU KNOW NOTHING

After you create some piece of collateral, don't look at it for a few days. Focus on other work or clear your mind over the weekend and forget what you created. When you take a look at it, have a more critical eye and ask yourself, "If I knew nothing about the product or service, would I understand this?" This is an iterative process that you need to go through several times.

Figure 12. Pretend you don't know anything about the product/service when you review your collateral

Each time you are reviewing your new collateral, try to clear your mind, and pretend you know nothing about your product or service. It is critical that you place yourself in a position that replicates that of your client. Assume they don't know what your offering is. Look at what you have created with virgin eyes every time you review it.

Crystal Clear: She remembers reading Marketing Simplified and that all the collateral that is created needs to echo the messaging statement. For her Sea Glas jewelry line, Crystal makes sure that the website pages reinforce the "Sea glass jewelry for every occasion" message. It shows different scenes of people wearing the jewelry at various places and at multiple times. Her social media posts repurpose the images, while modifying the text. When she attends the pop-up markets, the flyer she hands out shows the product along with her other jewelry. It emphasizes the versatility of the jewelry which can be worn at the beach, to a nightclub or out to a nice dinner.

OBTAIN FEEDBACK FROM OTHERS

It is also advisable to show your collateral to others in the company, loyal customers who will provide feedback, or individuals that you trust. Look for people who are both knowledgeable about your company and also others who are not aware about your product/service. Let them comment and provide feedback. Be open and vulnerable to their constructive criticism. In fact, encourage them to share their thoughts. You will likely receive different opinions from those aware of your product/services versus those who do not know much about it. Balance the feedback to improve your collateral.

. . .

Depending on what you are promoting, you could also put two or three options out on social media and have the audience vote or comment. If your company has an internal employee site you could also run a couple of ideas by a wider group. The bottom line is to consider the input from a variety of voices. When in doubt, simplify your collateral. You can always have more detailed information in specific documents. You don't need to say everything in every piece of collateral. The key is to have your potential customers realize quickly what it is you are offering and then have collateral for them to learn more via a variety of mediums. In the end you will deliver your message more effectively.

How much collateral you create will depend on your product or service, the resources, and the time and budget that you have. It is strongly recommended to prioritize your web page, videos and search collateral. Most products are discovered by search and your web site. Videos are growing in popularity as well and allow you more creative freedom. Make sure these items are clear to see on computers and tablets as well as mobile devices. The initial introduction of what you offer must be easy for potential clients to access and comprehended.

6

HERDING THE CATS

COMMUNICATING TO MANAGEMENT

After you have started developing the collateral, but before it is complete, it is time to begin herding the cats. What do I mean by herding the cats? It is an expression I use to align management and other groups or resources who will be supporting you. Mainly, herding the cats ensures everyone who is working with you understands their roles, action items and clear, specific responsibilities. Another aspect of this phrase is having the right mentality to execute the campaign deliverables. There will be numerous tasks that have to be accomplished and likely many people will be involved. Coordination and communication of your campaign is important.

. . .

The most valuable piece of information to communicate your campaign will be the swim lanes of the detailed marketing roll out. If you are sharing what you plan to do with executives and others, you should create a presentation which explains your goals, strategy and deliverables before jumping to the swim lanes' specific actions. If you have a boss or many bosses, you need to take the time to create this deck. As I mentioned earlier, I have created a template powerpoint file which you can use as a starting point for this type of meeting. This includes slides for your goals, messaging details and swim lane examples to save your time. Purchase this file through PayPal.

Click paypal.me/marketingsimplified/2.99 to send your payment and complete the transaction. The swim lane template PPT will save you time and make it easier to visualize and communicate your campaign. For only $2.99 the PowerPoint file will be emailed to your address.

Figure 13. Needs no explanation

My suggestion for a presentation to communicate to management/executives is to lead with your goals and then create a strategy statement. The goals are tangible. Goals are what we want to accomplish, and executives will want to know them. You already have goals. A strategy is how you plan on doing it. Strategy statements themselves are not measurable, but they are intended to generate action and show how you will market. They explain how you will achieve your goals. A typical strategy statement example could be, "We are going to leverage our other service to help us sell more of an existing product." Another example could be, "We will educate customers on the new product so they are aware we now have an offering in that market."

By creating a few higher level slides at the beginning, you will walk others through, in a logical fashion, what you intend to do. These introductory slides will help explain why you have chosen the goals of the campaign and how you plan to achieve them using the different mediums. The funnel diagram is often helpful to demonstrate that you have thought about what is required to ultimately achieve the goals. Once you have all of this explained, you can walk everyone through the swim lanes. If you have a piece of collateral or something that is reasonably far along, but still a work in progress, you can show that as an example. Just be up front that the collateral is still being developed and not final.

Once again, be open to feedback, suggestions and criticisms. Remember that some people may be looking at this plan for the first time, and they may need extra time to digest it. Once they understand the plan, their viewpoint may be valuable as it will likely differ from those of other, more seasoned, audience members. The goal of sharing the plan details is to allow everyone to understand it, and line up the resources necessary to make the campaign as successful as possible. If you are a small company, you might want to share your plan with complementary companies, those who do not directly compete with yours or individuals who can relate to your offerings. They may provide some feedback to improve your campaign.

Crystal Clear: For Crystal, aligning the company is relatively easy because it is a small organization. Still she runs her marketing plan by her brother who works in the business. She also shares it with very close friends and investors who helped her get the company off the ground. Crystal incorporates the feedback from this close knit group of individuals.

If you are in a larger organization, don't be surprised if you need multiple meetings to explain your campaign details, not only to the same people, but also to higher-ups in the organization. This can be scary if you are not confident in what you are rolling out. So, before you present your plan to a larger audience, make sure you have all your details understood. If you have done the goals, messaging, delivery and started work on the marketing collateral, then you will be well prepared. Look at these presentations as positive exposure for you to highlight your capabilities and skills. If you have done the work thus far, you should have confidence in what you present.

CONSTANTLY BIAS TOWARDS EXECUTION

After you have shared the campaign, you now need to execute. Focus on finishing the collateral (the collection of media assets that you will need). Certainly for the first several weeks of the campaign, you need to have everything completed before you start delivering. A warning from my work experience, just before a campaign kicks off, there will always be doubters. If you've gone through all of the details in this book thus far, you should be ready to go, but beware of those who will put the brakes on. In larger organizations, you will most likely have to sell harder internally than externally. There are several reasons why this might be the case.

Sometimes managers are driven by fear. Other executives would rather keep the status quo and not do anything new. The reality is that you have to be prepared to sell your campaign internally.

Inevitably, at the last minute someone will say they want something to be improved or changed. A few times I heard that my overall strategy was not good enough. Plan on incorporating specific suggestions that they think will improve the strategy. Some people expect over-the-top marketing strategies along the lines of something created by Steve Jobs. Understand that while a suggestion might be a small improvement, it will not warrant starting over. The goal at this stage is to execute. Your success depends on executing a marketing strategy. In my experience, the overwhelming number of strategies are going to have more or less the same effectiveness. The key is to execute. Those who execute have a much higher chance of success.

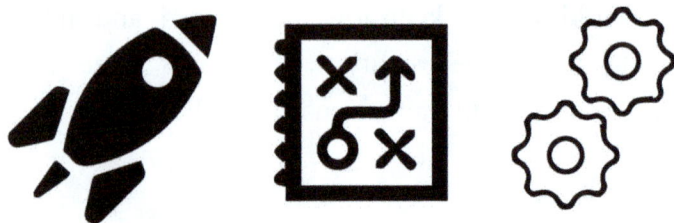

Figure 14. Execution is most important and often scares
many executives

My point is that execution is significantly more important than a grandiose idea or strategy. I once read that
execution eats strategy for lunch. Most people and
companies fail, not because of their ideas or strategies,
but because they did not execute. Always, always bias
towards execution and finishing the job. People who
pontificate and say you have to keep reworking a plan
or take more surveys or whatever are not being realistic.
If you have reviewed your campaign plan with multiple
people, and your management agrees, then you should
go forward. Recognize that sometimes managers and
people have hidden agendas they are worried about.
What if this fails? What if customers don't understand
and so on. The best thing you can do is communicate
the plan with the PowerPoint deck, and obtain the
minimal organizational alignment you need. If you have

done the work, don't contemplate your navel. Focus on finishing the collateral and delivering and executing your campaign.

7

DELIVERING

REPETITION IS KEY

Now that you have everything ready to go, the excitement and stress levels will build. It is normal for this to be the case when there are deadlines. Embrace the fact that a firm deadline, like a date, actually pushes people to execute. The key here is to knock off each of the initial deliverables. Focus on aligning what you need to get done for the launch date. Prioritize what you need to do, and help prioritize and set expectations for others who are working to create various collateral. Important early deliverables will likely include the web site, completing the press release, search criteria, FAQs, social posts, product flyers, how-to guides, videos, etc. All this should be in your swim lane plan. Use it as a guide to ensure all of the details you need to deliver are completed.

. . .

Keep in mind that, as you start your campaign, you will have to be patient. Remember that people need to see your message multiple times, maybe 6, 7 or more times before it sinks in. This is why I always recommend your plan to have an initial lightning event followed by rolling thunder. The initial press release, website page or event kicks everything off. This is the lighting. The rolling thunder is your consistent reinforcement and replaying of your messaging such as follow up social posts, more detailed documents, articles, ad placement, ect. Regularly delivering collateral that is in your swim lane plan will help your message sink in.

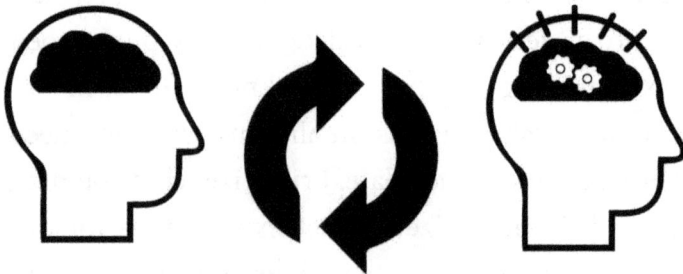

Figure 15. Repetition of your message is required

Crystal Clear: Crystal has decided to launch her new Sea Glas jewelry line at the largest pop-up market in town. Using the swim lane to coordinate her marketing efforts, she starts teasing out that a new line of products is coming in a couple weeks. She puts a countdown timer on her website and encourages people to visit her at the pop-up market for the reveal. After the initial event, she plans to release a video a week later. She uses pictures from the reveal for social media over the next several weeks and months. The webcast will be airing in a couple months and other activities will follow. All of these activities will reinforce her new "Sea glass jewelry for every occasion" message and promote the product line.

One area I'd like to bring up has to do with collateral that are designed for salespeople to use with customers. For example, if you have a demo unit or evaluation kit or something similar, it is critical that you package the solution correctly. What do I mean by that? Well, I'm drawing on my own experience when I was a field support engineer and a sales manager. It was always amazing to me when marketing delivered to us collateral that was overly complicated, poorly documented or simply not polished enough for customer consumption.

CAN SALES USE WHAT YOU DELIVER?

If you have to create something for salespeople, recognize a few things. Most sales forces don't typically have all the resources that a headquarters' location has. Don't assume your sales force has time to read a detailed guide, and remember they are likely not as up to speed on your product launch as you are. Given this status, what do you need to ensure success? There are two key items you must address.

First, make sure you send a complete package. Don't assume the sales office has anything other than the basics. One time we had our marketing team create a demo kit. They sent us an accessory board with instructions about how we had to use another hardware board that was sent 6 months before. Needless to say, we never actually did that demo. The hardware board we received months before was left with a customer who was evaluating it. Most other sales offices did not show the demo either. When I explained this dilemma to a marketing person, he was shocked. They put lots of work into the demo, but sales did not deliver it to customers broadly. The point is that you should send everything needed for the demo wherever possible.

Secondly, train your sales force. It is strongly suggested that you do multiple training sessions. I'm not just talking about holding two webinar sessions. Just like your customers need repetition to absorb your message, so do your sales people. You should do a live webinar-type training, and then travel to the field shortly after and do it in person. Better yet, have the sales person set up customer visits and do the demo then. Have each sales person first do the demo for you in a closed environment. Then encourage them to do the demo for your target customers. It is critical to have your sales force confident and comfortable.

To recap, your campaign should have all the key deliverables ready by the launch date, and remember that repetition will be needed for your message to sink in. If things start to slip, prioritize the most important items and just keep going. Execution is most important. Not everything may go according to plan, but focus and stay on schedule as much as possible. Moving the ball forward and continuing to deliver to your swim lane items will increase your odds of delivering a successful campaign.

8

MEASURING

WHAT ISN'T MEASURED ISN'T MANAGED

How do you know how your campaign is progressing? You measure it! I once heard that in business, what isn't measured, isn't managed. That is pretty spot on. Whatever marketing campaign you implement should have some method of measurement. If you recall, the first step is to create at least one goal. It is at the measuring step where you can start to see how your campaign is performing. Without any goals you would just be doing things with no idea if there is an impact or if you are wasting your time. Don't go crazy measuring, but do it periodically.

Whether you have decided to look at leads, web hits, page views, opportunities, visitors to your booth, customer visits, etc. make sure these are early indicators related to your ultimate goals. How often you review your goals is up to your judgement. It is common to review on a weekly, bi-weekly or monthly frequency, but this is based on campaigns I've run. The bottom line is, make sure you do measure and check your campaign progress. After all, a successful campaign might get you a raise or it should, at the minimum, raise your profile in the organization.

Crystal Clear: Crystal goes back to the first step of Marketing Simplified, which was to generate an additional 2500 website visitors and achieve $2500 per month in sales. Because she has real time sales data, she knows that all of her new Sea Glas line is sold out for the next few weeks. Four weeks after the initial reveal, she checks to see how many website visitors there are. This will not only be an indication for future sales, but also to see if her initial assumptions about the funnel were correct.

Crystal also checks the two different web search terms she used and has found that one is much more effective. For the next month, she decides to keep the good term and try a new one. By measuring several key data points, Crystal is well on her way to keeping the business growing.

Measuring is also important because you can begin

to see what kind of return you will earn on your marketing investment. You may be a small business and operating with very scarce resources. By measuring your campaign you will see what are the best mediums. This allows you to make intelligent decisions if you have to cut some aspects of the campaign. In larger organizations, you will want to know what the return on your marketing budget investment is yielding. The insights from measuring also help guide what you should focus on for future campaigns.

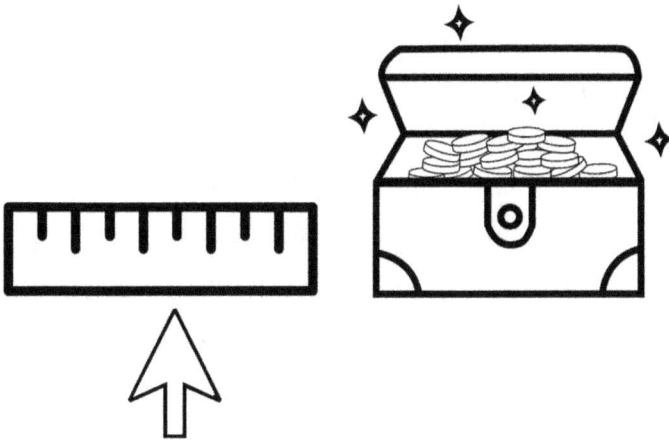

Figure 16. What isn't measured, isn't managed

You need to make sure you are following up with all of your leads and potential customers. I have seen salespeople who seem to be unaware of the need to follow up on qualified leads. Don't assume that the loop is being closed. You should also look to measure your conversion rate. How many prospects are turning into opportunities and ultimately converting to wins? One campaign we were running was able to attach points for the items that a prospect downloaded or for pages viewed. We set quite a high number before we converted the prospect into a lead. We purposely did this, so sales would see a very high percentage of the leads were of high quality.

Do what you can to have the leads be of higher quality initially. It is important that sales see the leads as having value. Once they are convinced, they are more likely to follow up. Taking these actions with sales will ensure the hard work you have put into messaging and the campaign will yield a more positive end result. Make sure you measure how your sales funnel is progressing on a regular basis. Knowing this conversion ratio will help you create better goals and focus your campaign for planning future marketing activities.

NOBODY BATS 1000%

Be advised that every campaign is not successful. The analogy can be made to baseball. No batter ever bats 1000%. Or in football, no quarterback ever completes 100% of his passes. Sometimes your product may not be right for the market or the times. Maybe your product is great, but the campaign is not hitting the mark. Or maybe you think you are selling trombone oil. I've experienced poorly trained sales people who are not able to close effectively. There could be a number of reasons. My advice is don't make drastic changes in the short term.

. . .

Remember your message takes time to sink in. After you have measured your campaign numbers a few times, determine how far off your goal you are. If you are within a small percentage, then maybe you just need to make some tweaks, like updates to the content or delivery medium. Another option would be to focus more energy on some of the swim lane actions that are performing better, and boost them up to make up for the other activities. Early in the campaign you have to resist the urge to make major changes. Stay the course and keep the effort going.

Continue to measure how things proceed. If, after longer periods of time, the progress towards your goal is not adequate, then you will need to make some changes. The length of time will depend on what the normal decision time is for your product or service. If you are selling a complex service which normally requires six months to close, then you should let your campaign play out for at least four months or more. At the end of this period, you will either have an acceptable number of leads and should keep the campaign going, if not, you will need to make changes.

Again, let the campaign play out for an extended period of time. How much time you will need is going to depend on several aspects, such as how expensive, complex, or easy to adopt as well as a host of other factors. I'd suggest not making any big changes for at least a couple months. Let your message sink in. Look at the early indicators in your sales funnel. Depending how far off you are will help dictate if you should make changes. If after a longer period of time it is clear you are far off your goals, then you should make changes. Remember the definition of insanity!

What you change will vary. Sometimes you only need to change your expectations. Maybe the goals you set were unrealistic. Perhaps they need to be scaled down. Or it could be that more time is needed to reach your results. Of course, it could be that your content is not being received because it is too technical or unclear. Reach out to sales people, potential customers, and leads that declined to convert to see if you can determine what is the issue. This should help you determine if it is the product/service, your collateral, messaging, trombone oil or something else that needs to be modified.

9

SUMMARY

If you have followed the Marketing Simplified steps I've outlined, you will have improved the odds your promotion will be a success. Writing this has been a personal struggle as I've spent countless hours translating in my mind what actions I took, why I did them and how to best explain what you should do. I'm convinced the Marketing Simplified steps can be of great assistance to many businesses and individuals. It is my pleasure to have invested my personal time to share this knowledge with you. Please post a positive review if you found any or all of this information useful. If you have any suggestions or comments, make sure you phrase them in the form of a compliment! LOL. Just kidding, please drop me an email with your feedback and comments if you want at marketingsimplified.book@gmail.com I'm also open to book signings or speak to your group or organization. If you liked my book, please let others know. Good luck to you on your exciting marketing journey!

REFERENCES

1. https://www.inc.com/jeff-haden/it-only-took-disneys-bob-iger-1-sentence-to-give-best-advice-youll-hear-today.html
2. https://cxl.com/blog/9-things-to-know-about-influencing-purchasing-decisions/
3. https://sproutsocial.com/insights/best-times-to-post-on-social-media/#find-times

ABOUT THE AUTHOR & THE CREATION OF MARKETING SIMPLIFIED

It began in school when others just started to treat me poorly simply because they were cruel, didn't know any better, were insecure themselves or for some other reason. Perhaps it was because I wore glasses, was overweight, awkward or simply did not "fit in." Whether it was verbal or physical abuse, it all took its toll. Whatever the reason, the little confidence I had was crushed by the time I became a senior in high school. Looking back, most people experience some type of difficulty socially in school. The individuals who don't are usually those who peak when they are a senior and the rest of their life is a disappointment. That wasn't going to happen to me.

One day during that senior school year, I decided to go into the library and look at self help books. I sat down and started reading "You Can Become the Person You Want to Be," by Robert Schuller. It was the first time I'd ever had someone tell me I could do it. "It" was whatever my dreams were. For the first time in my life, I also heard my inner voice speaking words of encouragement directly to me. This new knowledge became the trajectory to turn my confidence around. I'd rely on this inner voice to pick me up and get me through tough times. "You can do it" was a regular refrain that I told myself over and over again. Little by little my confidence grew.

There was another motivator that drove me to improve my grades in school. This was independent of the inner voice. The motivation was smelly carbide dust and sweaty, monotonous, tough physical labor punctuated by occasional metal splinters. My father's machine shop, in which I'd spent my summers working from the age of 11 or 12 became a driving force, compelling me towards a college degree. When I was a junior, my high school advisor told me that if I didn't raise my C grades, I wouldn't gain entrance into a good university. The motivation to avoid working in a machine shop, combined with my inner voice started me on an upward trajectory.

That inner voice sometimes would make up contests to keep me going. In college, I felt a strong sense of competition with the other students, many of whom I believed had advantages that I lacked. In order to increase my own motivation, I pictured myself partaking in an "Educational Olympics" of sorts with the hopes of America resting on my shoulders alone. I heard that I must go the extra mile to defend the USA and be the most successful I can be. Crazy, silly, ridiculous and kind of unbelievable, but this inner voice enabled this B student in high school to graduate with a 3.6 GPA Magna Cum Laude electrical engineering degree. A few years later I earned a 3.6 GPA MBA in marketing.

Because none of my family was in a high tech field, I had to forge my own career path. Despite the scores of people telling me there will be many job offers lined up for you when you get out of school, this was not the case. Fortunately I did receive an offer and my work career was underway. But all along the way, there were doubters. People let me know that this could not be done or that was impossible to do or I was not good enough to do something. Despites the ups and down, I forged ahead. Once, to convince a hiring manager to interview me, I sent a flower basket with a note simply saying, "I know I can do the job." I did indeed earn that job, but the doubters never seemed to go away.

To grow professionally required a physical relocation for the family and myself. Nobody ever thought I would go, but I did go. Once we settled in I noticed many other interesting behaviors. Working in many different organizations, over several years, I started learning the best practices to implement not just in business, sales and marketing aspects but also dealing with people and how to get the most out of a team. I also saw what not to do and how some things are really hard to stop doing. All along the way, the doubters persisted. All I did was to continue to focus, execute, work smarter, harder and push ahead.

Perhaps it has something to do with being named Ted. I know another person with the same name who shared with me that he had to fight tooth and nail for everything he has accomplished. Sounds very familiar.

The good news is all this self talk, hard work and persistence resulted in a valuable accumulation of marketing and sales knowledge. The passion I've found has resulted in a fulfilling career whose journey is not yet complete.

Let me share some specifics of my work history, so you have an idea of how my experience led to the knowledge which I'm sharing. I actually started my career as an electrical engineer. After designing several electronic hardware boards, I determined this job was not for me long term. Don't get me wrong, I liked it for a few years, but after doing multiple hardware designs, it was already becoming monotonous. I'm not saying that engineering positions are bad, in fact they are great for people who thrive on technical details, predictable iterations and focus. It was just not for me.

After talking to many people and a former co-worker, I started in a position as a field application engineer (FAE). A former mentor who I worked with transitioned to a FAE position and he recommended I do the same. He said my personality combined with my technical knowledge would be a good fit. That role was one I liked and I performed it well for several years. This was my first role interfacing directly to customers and it really launched me in the direction I ultimately ended up.

I became more interested in knowing more about customer interactions and business deals. It led me to want to go into sales and sales management. I'd been working side by side with sales for several years as an FAE and I knew I could do a sales management role. So the company I was working for allowed me to become a sales manager. At first my territory was small, but as I grew the business, my responsibilities and area grew along with me. At the peak of my sales director roles, I was running a $100 million region encompassing about ⅓ of North America.

I enjoyed sales for the most part and I was good at it, but I noticed my influence on the future of the organization was limited. Even though I had a large territory for the company, I was growing frustrated that key customer feedback was never getting incorporated into future products. Often I was told only customers in my markets needed particular features or capabilities. I knew this was not the case, it was just that I was speaking up, where other sales people were just selling. This led me to go into marketing and business development roles. It was the best way I could influence the larger organization.

My first marketing role was more focused on business development. I was responsible for working with other companies who could use our products and were complementary to our technology. It was great to see where the roadmap of other companies were heading and matching how our technology could improve their solution. Having this visibility also uncovered where applications were going. Visibility that our organization did not have before I executed this role.

It was in this role where I identified a solution for an existing product which it was never intended to implement. By working with my engineering partner, we opened an entire new market application for an existing product. For this discovery, we earned a patent which I'm very proud of. How many marketing professionals do you know that have a patent?

After doing this role successfully, I was asked to do a strategic marketing role. It was in this position where I was helping define our product roadmap. At this time, the company was struggling and wanted to modify what the future products would be. I worked with a product planning engineer and a product marketing manager to define a new type of device family. This expanded the markets that the company could go after. Needless to say, these products continue to be a significant revenue contributor to this day. No one will tell me the exact amount but it is in the tens of millions of dollars annually.

Having been exposed to all the elements of product marketing, I really got excited about performing that role. It allowed me to interface with sales which I really enjoyed. In addition, I enjoyed teaching the sales force how to sell and promote our products. I was fortunate to work with some great marketing directors and managers. My mind was like a sponge soaking up all types of ideas and strategies. Because I had been the recipient of marketing collateral in my sales roles, I had a unique perspective that no other marketing co-worker had. I often leveraged my sales experience to improve on every marketing program and campaign.

All of these roles helped me shape my messaging, goals, campaign ideas, etc. that enabled me to create and execute compelling marketing campaigns. The time required to synthesize all the actions necessary for a successful marketing campaign were not easy to simplify. After many months and years, I was able to finish! It has been very rewarding for me to share all of this experience in a concise manner with you.

SPECIAL ACKNOWLEDGMENT AND THANK YOU

There are numerous individuals I have come across in my life that I want to thank. I will just be using first names or nicknames to protect the innocent, hahahaha. First let me start with my family. To my wife Janet for being understanding, caring and supportive. There have been times when I did not appreciate the important things in life, but you were always there for me. I love being your partner. Our kids Enzo and Dante. You have provided us a crazy roller coaster ride of life. Continue to find your passion and pursue your happiness. We love you both and we know you can do great things once you make up your mind. We completely believe in you. My mother is no longer with us, but I know she would be beaming that I finished this book. To my father who showed me that hard work was important and Fran who has been supportive, patient and understanding to us all. Hugs to my sisters Sandra, Diana and Maria.

My friends who know me in a very unique way. First Johnny Boom and Janis. Thanks for being in our lives and laughing often with us. Chris and Nancy the demolisher. I appreciate you reminding me of my 410 score on a regular basis.

Work friends are numerous and if you are not mentioned it does not mean I don't like you, but these were the individuals who most shaped me. I'll go in roughly chronological order. A big thanks to all of the following. Hal who taught me how to sell to large corporations. Hugs to Caren for being so kind and introducing me to Janet. George X, who taught me that distribution has all the characteristics of a dog except loyalty. To Snowy, aka Steve D. Although your sales strategy of just wooing them never worked, I did learn many things about personalities, relationships and sales techniques. Cliffy introduced me to the concept of taking forever to make a decision. Roger who explained how distribution actually works. Sean R who was one of my top bosses. Thanks for believing in me and allowing me to flourish in my first marketing/business development role. Gordon who explained to me just how many details there were to tackle for a successful marketing campaign.

Bruce F who shared the magic of messaging with me. It was like a light bulb went on for me when you showed me that. I always appreciated the collaboration with you. To Sparkles who educated me on back end web tools, lead nurturing and insights that are available. Thanks for the collaboration and laughs Grant J. Glad to have earned the patent with you. Special thanks to Badman and Joy. We were the three amigos. I learned just how powerful synergy between complementary people can be. To Diane T who taught me that non verbal queues were extremely important to pick up and understand. Timmy Tom, for educating me on how to introduce new features into future products and challenging my marketing ideas. The other Ted, who complimented me on my marketing capabilities and introduced me to new technologies. Shak Daddy who had faith in me and often had to use capital to defend my actions. To brother Prem, Aniket and Manu. Thanks for accepting me into the Indian harem and explaining the culture which made me a better person. Let's get together soon and laugh our butts off.

CC who was one of my top bosses. You always believed in me and fought for me. It was also great how we complemented one another. For Z, thanks for coming around to trust me and my capabilities. Loreta and David for helping turn my ideas into great videos. To Erik, Ronni, Jason, Elle and Kris who shared many secrets of social media, blogs, web and communications with me. #treacherousbutfun. Amber, thanks for proofreading and providing helpful changes to make this the best book possible.

If you are not listed but think you should be, email me at marketingsimplified.book@gmail.com

Praise for

Marketing Simplified

"Impressive overall! This book provides practical and succinct tools to market your product or service. I appreciated Ted's emphasis on execution over strategy and incorporating different perspectives to improve how you promote. You can easily connect with the author as he demonstrates that you don't have to be a great writer to effectively market. Don't be frustrated not knowing what to do, just follow the extremely implementable steps in this book."

- Mona Eliassen. Entrepreneur, Founder Eliassen Group, Inc.

"Anyone can follow the steps in Marketing Simplified and take ownership to promote your product or service to the widest possible market. Ted immediately describes what you need to do. His personal story and all the knowledge he shares is worth far more than the price. Marketing Simplified is an excellent book."

- Wes McGee. Founder & CEO at IC/3 Executive Search Consultants LLC

"The most powerful marketing is almost always the simplest. Ted takes a very simple and pragmatic step-by-step approach to marketing. It is a quick, easy read yet powerful in its messaging. Bravo!."

- Naveed Sherwani, PhD. Chairman, co-founder of LeapFive, Rapid Silicon and Global Semiconductor Group.

"Marketing Simplified successfully provides a straightforward, comprehensive guide for you to excel in marketing. Backed by 25+ years in the industry, Marena gifts the reader advice and tools that you can instantly utilize despite your skill set or your own years of experience."

- Danielle DiVittorio. President, DiVittorio Architecture and Design

Ted J Marena is an award winning marketing and business development executive